I0797290

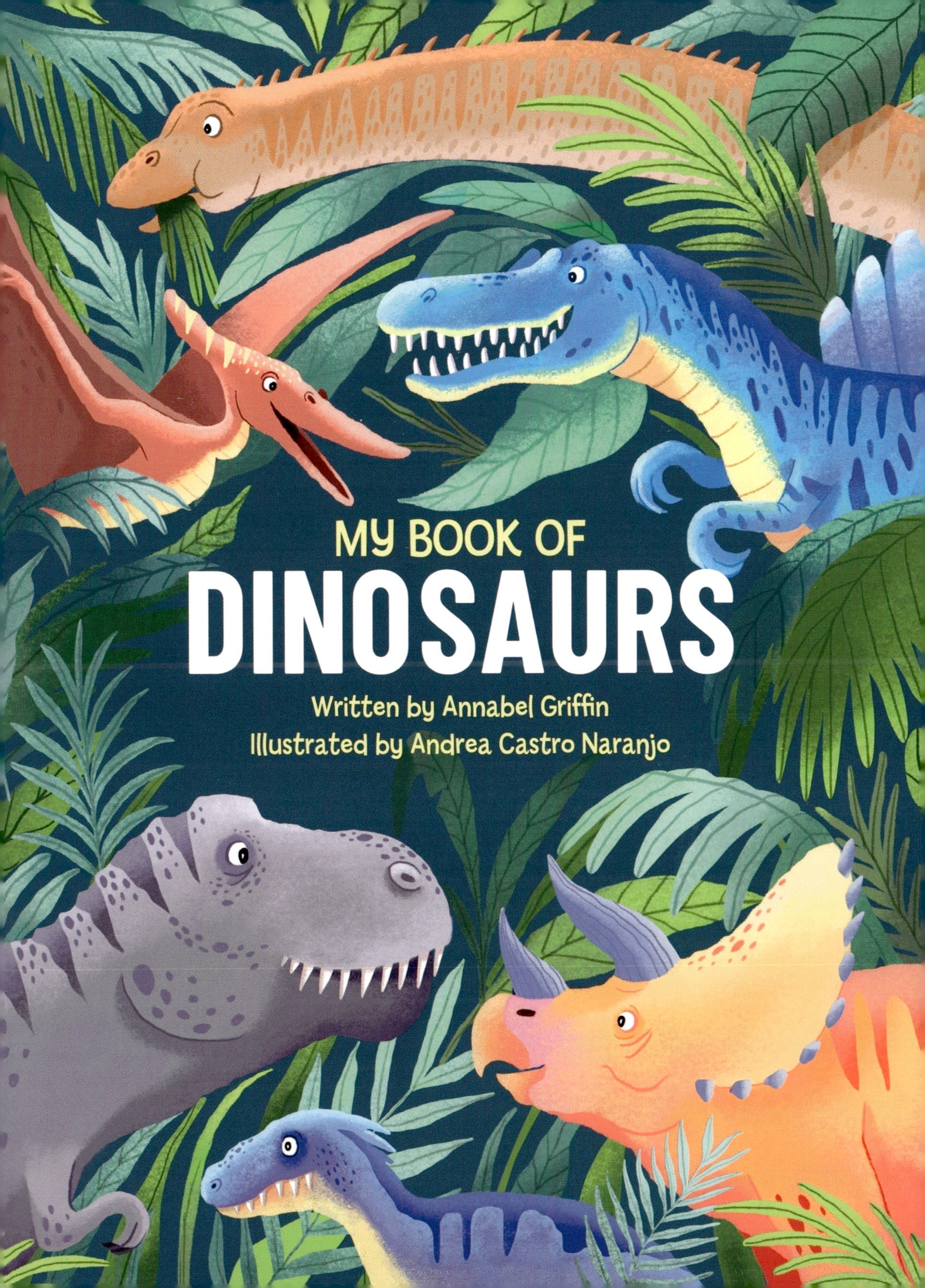
MY BOOK OF
DINOSAURS
Written by Annabel Griffin
Illustrated by Andrea Castro Naranjo

CONTENTS

First published in 2026 by Hungry Tomato Ltd
F15, Old Bakery Studios, Blewetts Wharf, Malpas Road, Truro, Cornwall,
TR1 1QH, UK.

A CIP catalog record for this book is available from the British Library.

ISBN 9781835694411

Manufactured in the USA

Discover more at
www.hungrytomato.com

Words in BOLD can be found in the glossary.

WHAT ARE DINOSAURS?

Dinosaurs were AWESOME!

There were lots of different types, from mighty meat-eating hunters, with sharp claws and teeth, to peaceful plant-eaters.

Long, long ago

They ruled the world millions of years ago, long before humans came on the scene. But not all types of dinosaurs were around at the same time.

Record breakers

The largest animals to ever walk on Earth were giant plant-eating dinosaurs. They stretched above the treetops and could weigh more than 14 elephants! Dinosaurs weren't all big though. Some were no bigger than a pigeon.

Did you know?

The word "dinosaur" means "terrible lizard". They were **reptiles**, just like the lizards, snakes and crocodiles that live on Earth today.

TYRANNOSAURUS REX

tie-RAN-oh-SORE-us rex

A FEROCIOUS hunter!

Tyrannosaurus rex, or T.rex for short, is one of the best known, and most feared, dinosaurs! This big, scary dinosaur hunted other dinosaurs, such as Triceratops.

Powerful tail
Strong legs
DID YOU KNOW?
I ate... meat. I was a **carnivore.**
I lived... 68-66 million years ago (late **Cretaceous period**).
I was found in... the USA and Canada.
This is how big I was:

STEGOSAURUS

STEG-oh-SORE-us

SLOW and STEADY!

Stegosaurus was a large dinosaur that lived in family groups. Scientists still aren't sure what the plates on its back were for. They might have been used for protection against **predators**.

DID YOU KNOW?

I ate… plants. I was a **herbivore**.

I lived… 155–145 million years ago (late **Jurassic period**).

I was found in… the USA and Portugal.

This is how big I was:

Large, bony plates
along its back
Tiny brain, the
size of a lime

TRICERATOPS

tri-SER-a-tops

Famous for its LARGE HORNS!

Triceratops was a similar size to an African elephant. Scientists think that its fancy neck frills were used to show off in front of other Triceratops. It lived at the same time as the T.rex.

Neck frill
Long horns
DID YOU KNOW?
I ate... plants. I was a herbivore.
I lived... 68-66 million years ago (late Cretaceous period).
I was found in... the USA.
This is how big I was:

SPINOSAURUS

SPINE-oh-SORE-us

Known for its POWERFUL jaws!

This snappy dinosaur might have been the longest ever meat-eating dinosaur. It probably lived near water and mostly ate fish. No one knows why it had the large "sail" on its back, but it might have been to attract other Spinosaurus, or to control its body heat.

Large "sail" along its spine
DID YOU KNOW?
I ate... mostly fish. I was a **piscivore**.
I lived... 100-93 million years ago (late Cretaceous period).
I was found in... North Africa.
This is how big I was:

VELOCIRAPTOR

vel-OSS-i-rap-tor

A speedy and athletic HUNTER!

Velociraptor was about the size of a wolf, but its bite was as strong as a lion's! It had a lot in common with modern-day birds but couldn't fly.

DID YOU KNOW?

I ate… meat. I was a carnivore.

I lived… 74–70 million years ago (late Cretaceous period).

I was found in… Mongolia and China.

This is how big I was:

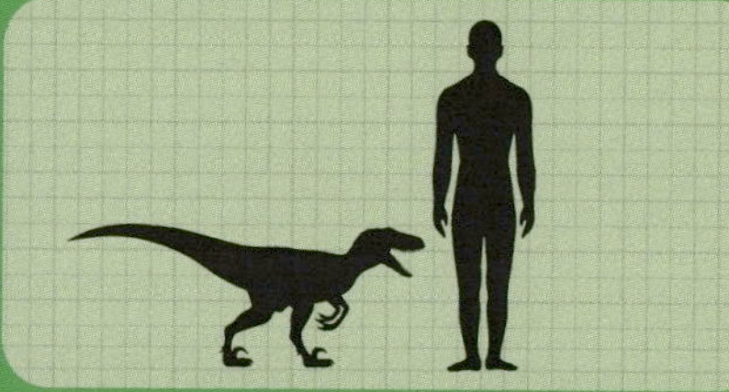

Covered in feathers
Razor-sharp teeth
Large attack claw
on each foot

DIPLODOCUS

dih-PLOD-uh-kus

This dinosaur was LONGER than a tennis court!

Diplodocus used its long neck to reach leaves from very tall trees, like giraffes do today. Its teeth were very weak and fell out once a month, so Diplodocus needed to keep growing new ones!

Long, whip-like tail
that could fight
off attackers
Spikes along neck,
back, and tail
DID YOU KNOW?
I ate... plants. I was a herbivore.
I lived... 155-145 million years ago
(late Jurassic period).
I was found in... the USA.
This is how big I was:

ANKYLOSAURUS

AN-kee-low-SORE-us

Bony plates for PROTECTION!

There was no messing with this dinosaur! It was covered in bony spikes and plates to protect its body from attack. Ankylosaurus could swing its heavy tail to defend itself from predators. It would have packed quite a punch!

Heavy club made of solid bone
DID YOU KNOW?
I ate... plants. I was a herbivore.
I lived... 74-67 million years ago (late Cretaceous period).
I was found in... the USA and Canada.
This is how big I was:

MORE GREAT DINOSAURS

Scientists have learned about so many fascinating dinosaurs that once lived all over the world. But they think there are still many more they haven't discovered yet!

ARCHAEOPTERYX (AR-kee-op-TE-rix)

This small bird-like dinosaur lived at the same time as Stegosaurus. Scientists believe that Archaeopteryx was able to fly, but probably not very far.

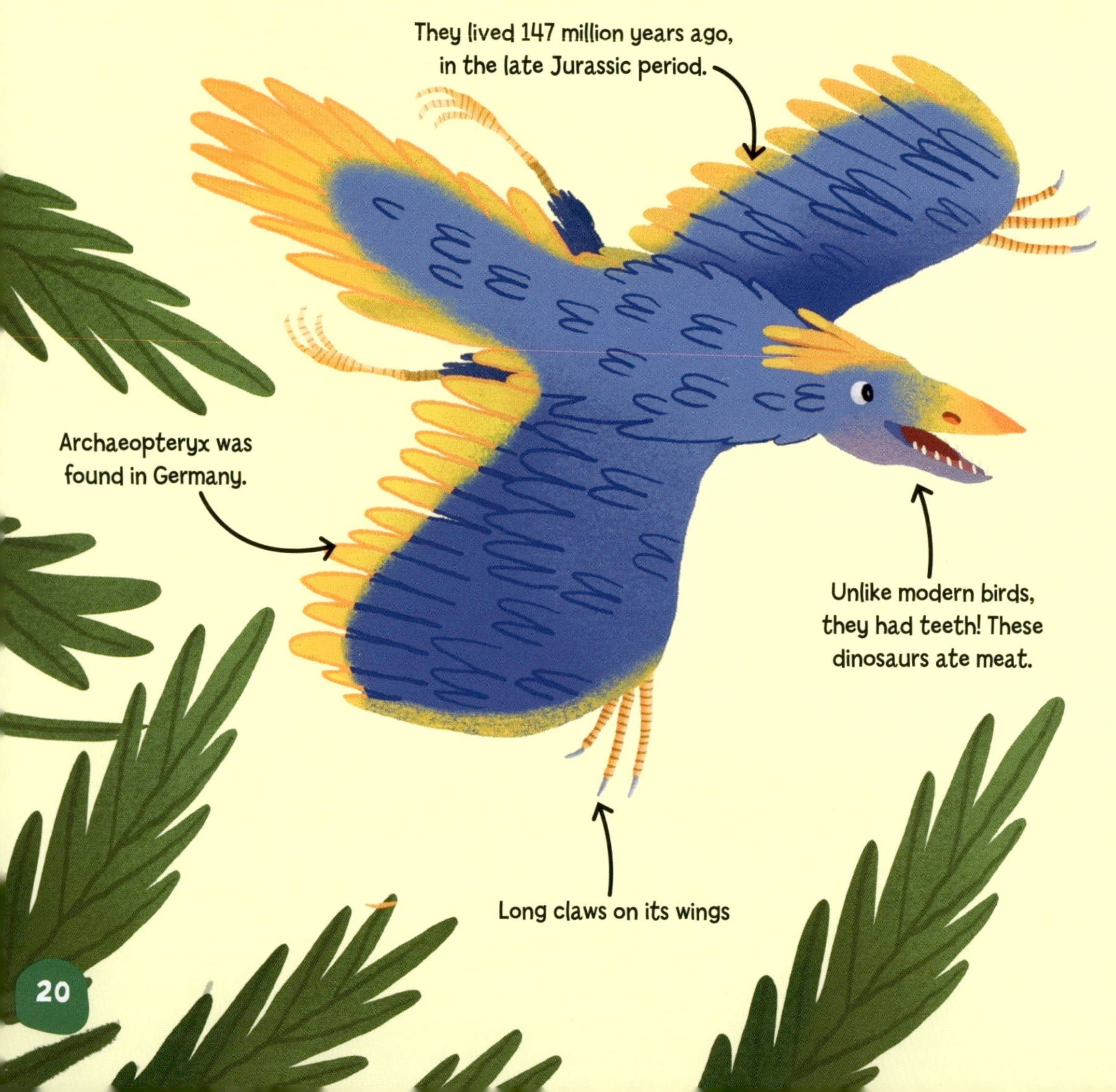

PARASAUROLOPHUS (PA-ra-saw-ROL-off-us)

The crest on this dinosaur's head was big and hollow. Scientists think it acted like a trumpet, giving Parasaurolophus a loud call for sending messages to its **herd**.

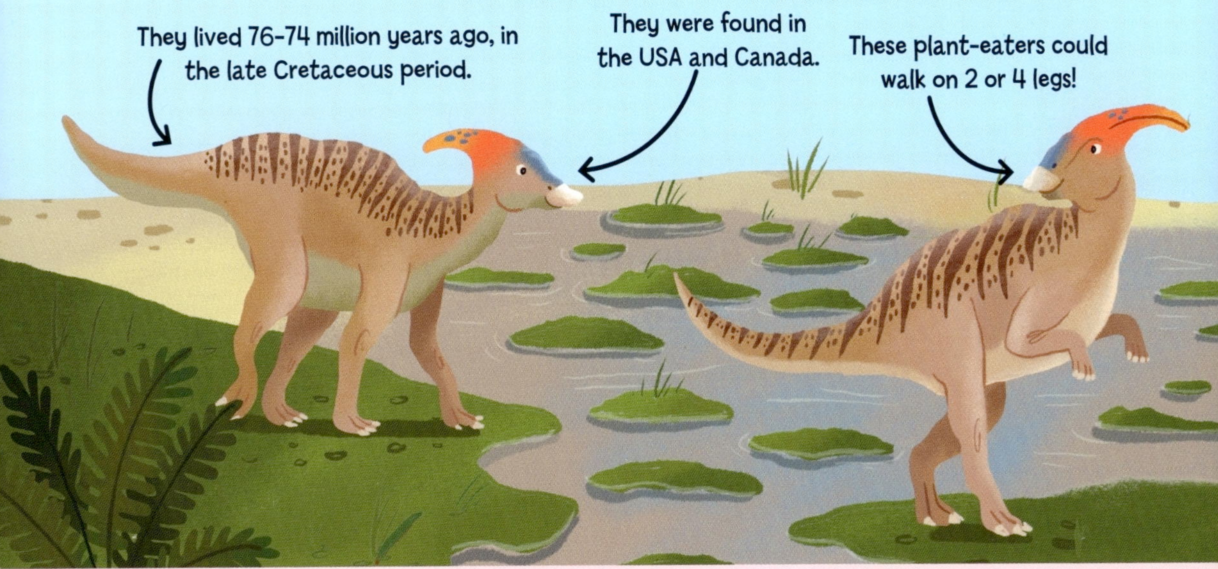

PACHYCEPHALOSAURUS (pack-ee-SEF-al-oh-SORE-us)

This dinosaur is famous for its thick, domed skull. Although it had a big head, its brain was tiny! No one knows what its thick skull was for, but one idea is that they butted heads with each other.

LIFE AFTER DINOSAURS

How do we know about dinosaurs?

The only reason we know about dinosaurs is because of fossils that have been discovered. Scientists can learn a lot from fossils, but there is still so much we don't know about dinosaurs.

What's a fossil?

Fossils are remains of dinosaurs like bones and teeth, or marks that they made like footprints. Fossils have been buried and **preserved** under layers of earth and rock for millions of years.

What happened to the dinosaurs?

Most scientists believe that Earth was hit by a giant **asteroid** 66 million years ago. The damage it caused killed off most of the big animals at the time, including dinosaurs.

Do dinosaurs still exist?

You won't see a giant T.rex walking on Earth today - thank goodness! But that doesn't mean all dinosaurs have completely disappeared. Believe it or not, modern birds are really living dinosaurs!

GLOSSARY

Asteroid - a chunk of rock that has fallen to Earth from space.

Carnivore - an animal that mostly eats meat.

Cretaceous period - a period of time that lasted from about 145 to 66 million years ago.

Herbivore - an animal that only eats plants.

Herd - a group of animals of one kind that live or travel together.

Jurassic period - a period of time that lasted from about 201 to 145 million years ago.

Piscivore - a type of carnivore (see left) that mostly eats fish.

Predators - animals that hunt and kill other animals for food.

Preserved - something that has been protected from harm, decay, or destruction.

Reptiles - a group of cold-blooded animals, including snakes, lizards, crocodiles, and dinosaurs.